THE LIFE OF JESUS—I AM

Retreat/Group Companion
WORKBOOK

RICHARD T. CASE

To my wife, Linda, who has faithfully walked with me and our family in understanding and receiving the Life of Jesus as the Great "I AM".

She has always been a faithful learner and receiver of the Names of God. She particularly had us spend time learning and receiving the depth of Christ's statements about Himself as the Great I AM"—

"I AM" THE BREAD OF LIFE,

"I AM" THE LIGHT OF THE WORLD,

"I AM" THE DOOR/GATE to ABUNDANT LIFE,

"I AM" THE GOOD SHEPHERD,

"I AM" THE RESURRECTION AND THE LIFE,

"I AM" THE WAY, THE TRUTH, AND THE LIFE,

"I AM" THE TRUE VINE.

Together, we studied and processed each statement and then applied the truths of who Christ is to our lives—as He then live this life out through us. It has been a joy to experience this and walk together into the profound truths of the Life of Christ. She is truly a woman of encouragement that seeks to enjoy the great "I AM".

Acknowledgments

We wish to thank all of the leaders of our **Ministry: Living Waters—ABIDE Ministries!** These leaders have also learned what it means to understand and receive the Life of the Great I AM: They have been shining examples of bearing witness to this life and giving this away to others—who then are learning to also explore and receive the Great "I AM".

These leaders are:

Jake & Mary Beckel
Rich & Janet Cocchiaro
Larry & Sherry Collet
Scott & Kristen Cornell
David & Melissa Dunkel
Tom & Susanne Ewing
Rick & Kelly Ferris
Joel & Christina Gunn
Rick & Nancy Hoover
Don & Rachelle Light
Chris and Heidi May
Steve & Carolyn Van Ooteghem
Preston & Lynda Pitts
Dan & Kathy Rocconi
Bob & Keri Rockwell
Allyson & Denny Weinberg

THE LIFE OF JESUS—I AM -COMPANION/RETREAT WORKBOOK
ABIDE MINISTRIES
7615 Lemon Gulch Way
Castle Rock, CO 80108

ISBN: 979-8-218-32048-5

Publisher's Cataloging-in-Publication data

Names:
Title:
Description: .
Identifiers: ISBN | LCCN
Subjects:

Printed in the United States of America 2023 — 1st ed

TABLE OF CONTENTS

INTRODUCTION

Read John 20:30–31:

The Purpose of This Book
[30] Now Jesus did many other signs in the presence of the disciples, which are not written in this book; [31] but these are written so that you may believe that Jesus is the Christ, the Son of God, and that by believing you may have life in his name.

____

____

____

____

____

Read John 8:54–59:

[54] Jesus answered, "If I glorify myself, my glory is nothing. It is my Father who glorifies me, of whom you say, 'He is our God.'[a] [55] But you have not known him. I know him. If I were to say that I do not know him, I would be a liar like you, but I do know him and I keep his word. [56] Your father Abraham rejoiced that he would see my day. He saw it and was glad." [57] So the Jews said to him, "You are not yet fifty years old, and have you seen Abraham?"[b] [58] Jesus said to them, "Truly, truly, I say to you, before Abraham was, I am." [59] So they picked up stones to throw at him, but Jesus hid himself and went out of the temple.

____

____

____

____

INTRODUCTION

Read Exodus 3:12–18:

[12] He said, "But I will be with you, and this shall be the sign for you, that I have sent you: when you have brought the people out of Egypt, you shall serve God on this mountain."

[13] Then Moses said to God, "If I come to the people of Israel and say to them, 'The God of your fathers has sent me to you,' and they ask me, 'What is his name?' what shall I say to them?" [14] God said to Moses, "I AM WHO I AM."[a] And he said, "Say this to the people of Israel: 'I AM has sent me to you.'" [15] God also said to Moses, "Say this to the people of Israel: 'The LORD,[b] the God of your fathers, the God of Abraham, the God of Isaac, and the God of Jacob, has sent me to you.' This is my name forever, and thus I am to be remembered throughout all generations. [16] Go and gather the elders of Israel together and say to them, 'The LORD, the God of your fathers, the God of Abraham, of Isaac, and of Jacob, has appeared to me, saying, "I have observed you and what has been done to you in Egypt, [17] and I promise that I will bring you up out of the affliction of Egypt to the land of the Canaanites, the Hittites, the Amorites, the Perizzites, the Hivites, and the Jebusites, a land flowing with milk and honey."' [18] And they will listen to your voice, and you and the elders of Israel shall go to the king of Egypt and say to him, 'The LORD, the God of the Hebrews, has met with us; and now, please let us go a three days' journey into the wilderness, that we may sacrifice to the LORD our God.'

____

____

____

____

____

Read Matthew 14:22–33:

Jesus Walks on the Water

[22] Immediately he made the disciples get into the boat and go before him to the other side, while he dismissed the crowds. [23] And after he had dismissed the crowds, he went up on the mountain by himself to pray. When evening came, he was there alone, [24] but the boat by this time was a long way[a] from the land,[b] beaten by the waves, for the wind was against them. [25] And in the fourth watch of the night[c] he came to them, walking on the sea. [26] But when the disciples saw him walking on the sea, they were terrified, and said, "It is a ghost!" and they cried out in fear. [27] But immediately Jesus spoke to them, saying, "Take heart; it is I. Do not be afraid."

[28] And Peter answered him, "Lord, if it is you, command me to come to you on the water." [29] He said, "Come." So Peter got out of the boat and walked on the water and came to Jesus. [30] But when he saw the wind,[d] he was afraid, and beginning to sink he cried out, "Lord, save me." [31] Jesus immediately reached out his hand and took hold of him, saying to him, "O you of little faith, why did you doubt?" [32] And when they got into the boat, the wind ceased. [33] And those in the boat worshiped him, saying, "Truly you are the Son of God."

INTRODUCTION

> **Read Hebrews 11:6:**
>
> [6] And without faith it is impossible to please him, for whoever would draw near to God must believe that he exists and that he rewards those who seek him.

> "Jesus supernaturally fed the 5,000 through multiplying it in the baskets He's just demonstrated that the spiritual supersedes the physical—and that He can do remarkable things."

The Bread of Life:

Jesus referred to Himself as the Bread of Life. What does that mean? What then are we to do with this bread? How do we fulfill this? Why is this so crucial to how we live out His life in us?

Read John 6:22–40; 47–51:

I Am the Bread of Life

22 On the next day the crowd that remained on the other side of the sea saw that there had been only one boat there, and that Jesus had not entered the boat with his disciples, but that his disciples had gone away alone. 23 Other boats from Tiberias came near the place where they had eaten the bread after the Lord had given thanks. 24 So when the crowd saw that Jesus was not there, nor his disciples, they themselves got into the boats and went to Capernaum, seeking Jesus.

25 When they found him on the other side of the sea, they said to him, "Rabbi, when did you come here?" 26 Jesus answered them, "Truly, truly, I say to you, you are seeking me, not because you saw signs, but because you ate your fill of the loaves. 27 Do not work for the food that perishes, but for the food that endures to eternal life, which the Son of Man will give to you. For on him God the Father has set his seal." 28 Then they said to him, "What must we do, to be doing the works of God?" 29 Jesus answered them, "This is the work of God, that you believe in him whom he has sent." 30 So they said to him, "Then what sign do you do, that we may see and believe you? What work do you perform? 31 Our fathers ate the manna in the wilderness; as it is written, 'He gave them bread from heaven to eat.'" 32 Jesus then said to them, "Truly, truly, I say to you, it was not Moses who gave you the bread from heaven,

but my Father gives you the true bread from heaven. [33] For the bread of God is he who comes down from heaven and gives life to the world." [34] They said to him, "Sir, give us this bread always."

[35] Jesus said to them, "I am the bread of life; whoever comes to me shall not hunger, and whoever believes in me shall never thirst. [36] But I said to you that you have seen me and yet do not believe. [37] All that the Father gives me will come to me, and whoever comes to me I will never cast out. [38] For I have come down from heaven, not to do my own will but the will of him who sent me. [39] And this is the will of him who sent me, that I should lose nothing of all that he has given me, but raise it up on the last day. [40] For this is the will of my Father, that everyone who looks on the Son and believes in him should have eternal life, and I will raise him up on the last day."

[47] Truly, truly, I say to you, whoever believes has eternal life. [48] I am the bread of life. [49] Your fathers ate the manna in the wilderness, and they died. [50] This is the bread that comes down from heaven, so that one may eat of it and not die. [51] I am the living bread that came down from heaven. If anyone eats of this bread, he will live forever. And the bread that I will give for the life of the world is my flesh."

What is the connection between the manna provided every day in the wilderness and Jesus as the bread of life? What are we to do with this bread? When and why?

Read Deuteronomy 8:1–10:

Remember the Lord Your God

8 "The whole commandment that I command you today you shall be careful to do, that you may live and multiply, and go in and possess the land that the LORD swore to give to your fathers. [2] And you shall remember the whole way that the LORD your God has led you these forty years in the wilderness, that he might humble you, testing you to know what was in your heart, whether you would keep his commandments or not. [3] And he humbled you and let you hunger and fed you with manna, which you did not know, nor did your fathers know, that he might make you know that man does not live by bread alone, but man lives by every word[a] that comes from the mouth of the LORD. [4] Your clothing did not wear out on you and your foot did not swell these forty years. [5] Know then in your heart that, as a man disciplines his son, the LORD your God disciplines you. [6] So you shall keep the commandments of the LORD your God by walking in his ways and by fearing him. [7] For the LORD your God is bringing you into a good land, a land of brooks of water, of fountains and springs, flowing out in the valleys and hills, [8] a land of wheat and barley, of vines and fig trees and pomegranates, a land of olive trees and honey, [9] a land in which you will eat bread without scarcity, in which you will lack nothing, a land whose stones are iron, and out of whose hills you can dig copper. [10] And you shall eat and be full, and you shall bless the LORD your God for the good land he has given you.

What was the purpose of the Passover? Why did God want the Israelites to remember and perform Passover every year? Associated with Passover is the Feast of Tabernacles—what is this? Why do these two feasts go together? How are we then to live these out now as believers?

Read Deuteronomy 16:1–17:

Passover

16 "Observe the month of Abib and keep the Passover to the LORD your God, for in the month of Abib the LORD your God brought you out of Egypt by night. [2] And you shall offer the Passover sacrifice to the LORD your God, from the flock or the herd, at the place that the LORD will choose, to make his name dwell there. [3] You shall eat no leavened bread with it. Seven days you shall eat it with unleavened bread, the bread of affliction—for you came out of the land of Egypt in haste—that all the days of your life you may remember the day when you came out of the land of Egypt. [4] No leaven shall be seen with you in all your territory for seven days, nor shall any of the flesh that you sacrifice on the evening of the first day remain all night until morning. [5] You may not offer the Passover sacrifice within any of your towns that the LORD your God is giving you, [6] but at the place that the LORD your God will choose, to make his name dwell in it, there you shall offer the Passover sacrifice, in the evening at sunset, at the time you came out of Egypt. [7] And you shall cook it and eat it at the place that the LORD your God will choose. And in the morning you shall turn and go to your tents. [8] For six days you shall eat unleavened bread, and on the seventh day there shall be a solemn assembly to the LORD your God. You shall do no work on it.

The Feast of Weeks

[9] "You shall count seven weeks. Begin to count the seven weeks from the time the sickle is first put to the standing grain. [10] Then you shall keep the Feast of Weeks to the LORD your God with the tribute of a freewill offering from your hand, which you shall give as the LORD your God blesses you. [11] And you shall rejoice before the LORD your God, you and your son and your daughter, your male servant and your female servant, the Levite who is within your towns, the sojourner, the fatherless, and the widow who are among you, at the place that the LORD your God will choose, to make his name dwell there. [12] You shall remember that you were a slave in Egypt; and you shall be careful to observe these statutes.

The Feast of Booths

[13] "You shall keep the Feast of Booths seven days, when you have gathered in the produce from your threshing floor and your winepress. [14] You shall rejoice in your feast, you and your son and your daughter, your male servant and your female servant, the Levite, the sojourner, the fatherless, and the widow who are within your towns. [15] For seven days you shall keep the feast to the LORD your God at the place that the LORD will choose, because the LORD your God will bless you in all your produce and in all the work of your hands, so that you will be altogether joyful.

[16] "Three times a year all your males shall appear before the LORD your God at the place that he will choose: at the Feast of Unleavened Bread, at the Feast of Weeks, and at the Feast of Booths. They shall not appear before the LORD empty-handed. [17] Every man shall give as he is able, according to the blessing of the LORD your God that he has given you.

How did Jesus more fully define the Passover? What then is the purpose of us taking communion regularly? What are we to understand as we take communion regularly? Why?

> **Read Matthew 26:26–29:**
>
> Institution of the Lord's Supper
> 26 Now as they were eating, Jesus took bread, and after blessing it broke it and gave it to the disciples, and said, "Take, eat; this is my body." 27 And he took a cup, and when he had given thanks he gave it to them, saying, "Drink of it, all of you, 28 for this is my blood of the[a] covenant, which is poured out for many for the forgiveness of sins. 29 I tell you I will not drink again of this fruit of the vine until that day when I drink it new with you in my Father's kingdom."

____

____

____

____

____

In light of what we are learning about the bread of life, what did Jesus mean when we are to ask for this day, our daily bread? How are we then to receive this daily? Why is this so important?

Read Luke 11:1–4:

The Lord's Prayer
11 Now Jesus[a] was praying in a certain place, and when he finished, one of his disciples said to him, "Lord, teach us to pray, as John taught his disciples." [2] And he said to them, "When you pray, say:

"Father, hallowed be your name.
Your kingdom come.
[3] Give us each day our daily bread,[b]
[4] and forgive us our sins,
    for we ourselves forgive everyone who is indebted to us.
And lead us not into temptation."

The Light of the World:

What does it mean when Jesus says, "He is the Light of the World?" What is the value and purpose of light? What then is important for us to live in this light? Why?

Read John 8:12–30:

I Am the Light of the World

12 Again Jesus spoke to them, saying, "I am the light of the world. Whoever follows me will not walk in darkness, but will have the light of life." 13 So the Pharisees said to him, "You are bearing witness about yourself; your testimony is not true." 14 Jesus answered, "Even if I do bear witness about myself, my testimony is true, for I know where I came from and where I am going, but you do not know where I come from or where I am going. 15 You judge according to the flesh; I judge no one. 16 Yet even if I do judge, my judgment is true, for it is not I alone who judge, but I and the Father[a] who sent me. 17 In your Law it is written that the testimony of two people is true. 18 I am the one who bears witness about myself, and the Father who sent me bears witness about me." 19 They said to him therefore, "Where is your Father?" Jesus answered, "You know neither me nor my Father. If you knew me, you would know my Father also." 20 These words he spoke in the treasury, as he taught in the temple; but no one arrested him, because his hour had not yet come.

21 So he said to them again, "I am going away, and you will seek me, and you will die in your sin. Where I am going, you cannot come." 22 So the Jews said, "Will he kill himself, since he says, 'Where I am going, you cannot come'?" 23 He said to them, "You are from below; I am from above. You are of this world; I am not of this world. 24 I told you that you would die in your sins, for unless you believe that I am he you will die in your sins." 25 So they said to him, "Who are you?" Jesus said to them, "Just what I have been telling you from the beginning. 26 I have much to say about you and much to judge, but he who sent me is true, and I declare to the world what I have heard from him." 27 They did not understand that he had been speaking to them about the Father. 28 So Jesus said to them, "When you have lifted up the Son of Man, then you will know that I am he, and that I do nothing on my own authority, but speak just as the

Father taught me. [29] And he who sent me is with me. He has not left me alone, for I always do the things that are pleasing to him." [30] As he was saying these things, many believed in him.

The tabernacle was also called the Tent of Meeting—where the Israelites could meet with and talk with God. In the tabernacle, there was always to be what? How was this to be kept functioning? How does the oil needed for the light to burn relate to us as believers? How are we to operate in the same way? Why?

Read Exodus 27:20–21:

Oil for the Lamp
[20] "You shall command the people of Israel that they bring to you pure beaten olive oil for the light, that a lamp may regularly be set up to burn. [21] In the tent of meeting, outside the veil that is before the testimony, Aaron and his sons shall tend it from evening to morning before the LORD. It shall be a statute forever to be observed throughout their generations by the people of Israel.

What does Daniel reveal is associated with the light? What does that mean for us? How are we to walk with God in the light to receive these benefits? Why is this so important for us?

Read Daniel 2:20–23:

[20] Daniel answered and said:
"Blessed be the name of God forever and ever,
    to whom belong wisdom and might.
[21] He changes times and seasons;
    he removes kings and sets up kings;
he gives wisdom to the wise
    and knowledge to those who have understanding;
[22] he reveals deep and hidden things;
    he knows what is in the darkness,
    and the light dwells with him.
[23] To you, O God of my fathers,
    I give thanks and praise,
for you have given me wisdom and might,
    and have now made known to me what we asked of you,
    for you have made known to us the king's matter."

What does light do? What then is important for us as we face the darkness of the world? Why?

> **Read John 1:4–5:**
>
> [4] In him was life,[a] and the life was the light of men. [5] The light shines in the darkness, and the darkness has not overcome it.

____

____

____

____

____

Paul describes that Jesus is the light and says that this reflected in Christ's good confession. From the following two verses, what is the good confession? What does that mean for how we live? Why?

> **Read 1 Timothy 6:13–16:**
>
> [13] I charge you in the presence of God, who gives life to all things, and of Christ Jesus, who in his testimony before[a] Pontius Pilate made the good confession, [14] to keep the commandment unstained and free from reproach until the appearing of our Lord Jesus Christ, [15] which he will display at the proper time—he who is the blessed and only Sovereign, the King of kings and Lord of lords, [16] who alone has immortality, who dwells in unapproachable light, whom no one has ever seen or can see. To him be honor and eternal dominion. Amen.

____

____

____

____

Read John 18:19–38:

The High Priest Questions Jesus

[19] The high priest then questioned Jesus about his disciples and his teaching. [20] Jesus answered him, "I have spoken openly to the world. I have always taught in synagogues and in the temple, where all Jews come together. I have said nothing in secret. [21] Why do you ask me? Ask those who have heard me what I said to them; they know what I said." [22] When he had said these things, one of the officers standing by struck Jesus with his hand, saying, "Is that how you answer the high priest?" [23] Jesus answered him, "If what I said is wrong, bear witness about the wrong; but if what I said is right, why do you strike me?" [24] Annas then sent him bound to Caiaphas the high priest.

Peter Denies Jesus Again

[25] Now Simon Peter was standing and warming himself. So they said to him, "You also are not one of his disciples, are you?" He denied it and said, "I am not." [26] One of the servants of the high priest, a relative of the man whose ear Peter had cut off, asked, "Did I not see you in the garden with him?" [27] Peter again denied it, and at once a rooster crowed.

Jesus Before Pilate

[28] Then they led Jesus from the house of Caiaphas to the governor's headquarters.[a] It was early morning. They themselves did not enter the governor's headquarters, so that they would not be defiled, but could eat the Passover. [29] So Pilate went outside to them and said, "What accusation do you bring against this man?" [30] They answered him, "If this man were not doing evil, we would not have delivered him over to you." [31] Pilate said to them, "Take him yourselves and judge him by your own law." The Jews said to him, "It is not lawful for us to put anyone to death." [32] This was to fulfill the word that Jesus had spoken to show by what kind of death he was going to die.

My Kingdom Is Not of This World

[33] So Pilate entered his headquarters again and called Jesus and said to him, "Are you the King of the Jews?" [34] Jesus answered, "Do you say this of your own accord, or did others say it to you about me?" [35] Pilate answered, "Am I a Jew? Your own nation and the chief priests have delivered you over to me. What have you done?" [36] Jesus answered, "My kingdom is not of this world. If my

kingdom were of this world, my servants would have been fighting, that I might not be delivered over to the Jews. But my kingdom is not from the world." [37] Then Pilate said to him, "So you are a king?" Jesus answered, "You say that I am a king. For this purpose I was born and for this purpose I have come into the world—to bear witness to the truth. Everyone who is of the truth listens to my voice." [38] Pilate said to him, "What is truth?"

After he had said this, he went back outside to the Jews and told them, "I find no guilt in him.

____

____

____

____

____

LESSON 1:
"I AM" THE LIGHT OF THE WORLD

When you come to the light, you are to come to truth. What then is truth, and how do we stay in the light? Why is this so important to how we live?

Read John 3:16–21:

For God So Loved the World

16 "For God so loved the world,[a] that he gave his only Son, that whoever believes in him should not perish but have eternal life. 17 For God did not send his Son into the world to condemn the world, but in order that the world might be saved through him. 18 Whoever believes in him is not condemned, but whoever does not believe is condemned already, because he has not believed in the name of the only Son of God. 19 And this is the judgment: the light has come into the world, and people loved the darkness rather than the light because their works were evil. 20 For everyone who does wicked things hates the light and does not come to the light, lest his works should be exposed. 21 But whoever does what is true comes to the light, so that it may be clearly seen that his works have been carried out in God."

____

____

____

____

____

LESSON 2:
"I AM" THE DOOR/GATE TO ABUNDANT LIFE

"I am" is God—all of God and all that we need for all of life."

The Gate:

From the following four verses: What are the functions of a gate? How does Jesus fulfill these functions? What are the benefits to us who go through the gate? What does that mean for how we then relate to the gate? Why is this so important for us to understand for the fullness of our life?

Read John 10:7–10:

[7] So Jesus again said to them, "Truly, truly, I say to you, I am the door of the sheep. [8] All who came before me are thieves and robbers, but the sheep did not listen to them. [9] I am the door. If anyone enters by me, he will be saved and will go in and out and find pasture. [10] The thief comes only to steal and kill and destroy. I came that they may have life and have it abundantly.

LESSON 2:
"I AM" THE DOOR/GATE TO ABUNDANT LIFE

Read Psalm 24:7–10:

7 Lift up your heads, O gates!
  And be lifted up, O ancient doors,
  that the King of glory may come in.
8 Who is this King of glory?
  The Lord, strong and mighty,
  the Lord, mighty in battle!
9 Lift up your heads, O gates!
  And lift them up, O ancient doors,
  that the King of glory may come in.
10 Who is this King of glory?
  The Lord of hosts,
  he is the King of glory! *Selah*

Read Psalm 118:19–20:

19 Open to me the gates of righteousness,
  that I may enter through them
  and give thanks to the LORD.
20 This is the gate of the LORD;
  the righteous shall enter through it.

Read Isaiah 26:1–4:

You Keep Him in Perfect Peace

26 In that day this song will be sung in the land of Judah:

"We have a strong city;

    he sets up salvation

    as walls and bulwarks.

² Open the gates,

    that the righteous nation that keeps faith may enter in.

³ You keep him in perfect peace

    whose mind is stayed on you,

    because he trusts in you.

⁴ Trust in the LORD forever,

    for the LORD GOD is an everlasting rock.

LESSON 2:
"I AM" THE DOOR/GATE TO ABUNDANT LIFE

As we seek God's will, we are to listen, watch, and wait. The waiting is at the gate. What happened at the gate and thus, what does this mean to wait there? For what are we waiting? If we wait, what will be given? Why is this so critical to live out our life in Christ?

Read Proverbs 8:32–35:

32 "And now, O sons, listen to me:
　　blessed are those who keep my ways.
33 Hear instruction and be wise,
　　and do not neglect it.
34 Blessed is the one who listens to me,
　　watching daily at my gates,
　　waiting beside my doors.
35 For whoever finds me finds life
　　and obtains favor from the LORD,

The good shepherd:

What does a good shepherd do? What is crucial for us as sheep then to follow the good shepherd? What does that mean as to how we walk with God? Why is this so important for us to learn and experience?

Read John 10:1–5; 1–18; 25–30:

I Am the Good Shepherd

10 "Truly, truly, I say to you, he who does not enter the sheepfold by the door but climbs in by another way, that man is a thief and a robber. [2] But he who enters by the door is the shepherd of the sheep. [3] To him the gatekeeper opens. The sheep hear his voice, and he calls his own sheep by name and leads them out. [4] When he has brought out all his own, he goes before them, and the sheep follow him, for they know his voice. [5] A stranger they will not follow, but they will flee from him, for they do not know the voice of strangers."

I Am the Good Shepherd

10 "Truly, truly, I say to you, he who does not enter the sheepfold by the door but climbs in by another way, that man is a thief and a robber. [2] But he who enters by the door is the shepherd of the sheep. [3] To him the gatekeeper opens. The sheep hear his voice, and he calls his own sheep by name and leads them out. [4] When he has brought out all his own, he goes before them, and the sheep follow him, for they know his voice. [5] A stranger they will not follow, but they will flee from him, for they do not know the voice of strangers." [6] This figure of speech Jesus used with them, but they did not understand what he was saying to them.

[7] So Jesus again said to them, "Truly, truly, I say to you, I am the door of the sheep. [8] All who came before me are thieves and robbers, but the sheep did not listen to them. [9] I am the door. If anyone enters by me, he will be saved and will go in and out and find pasture. [10] The thief comes only to steal and kill and destroy. I came that they may have life and have it abundantly. [11] I am the good shepherd. The good shepherd lays down his life for the sheep. [12] He who is a hired hand and not a shepherd, who does not own the sheep, sees the wolf coming and leaves the sheep and flees, and the wolf snatches them and scatters them. [13] He flees because he is a hired hand and cares nothing

for the sheep. [14] I am the good shepherd. I know my own and my own know me, [15] just as the Father knows me and I know the Father; and I lay down my life for the sheep. [16] And I have other sheep that are not of this fold. I must bring them also, and they will listen to my voice. So there will be one flock, one shepherd. [17] For this reason the Father loves me, because I lay down my life that I may take it up again. [18] No one takes it from me, but I lay it down of my own accord. I have authority to lay it down, and I have authority

[25] Jesus answered them, "I told you, and you do not believe. The works that I do in my Father's name bear witness about me, [26] but you do not believe because you are not among my sheep. [27] My sheep hear my voice, and I know them, and they follow me. [28] I give them eternal life, and they will never perish, and no one will snatch them out of my hand. [29] My Father, who has given them to me,[a] is greater than all, and no one is able to snatch them out of the Father's hand. [30] I and the Father are one."

From the following two verses: The Lord is MY shepherd. The "my" means it is personal. Thus, what are all the promises given to you personally from the shepherd? What do each of the promises mean? How then shall we live out this life as sheep under the leadership of the Shepherd? Why is this so important for us?

Read Psalm 23:1–6:

The LORD Is My Shepherd
A Psalm of David.
23 The LORD is my shepherd; I shall not want.
2   He makes me lie down in green pastures.
He leads me beside still waters.[a]
3   He restores my soul.
He leads me in paths of righteousness[b]
   for his name's sake.
4 Even though I walk through the valley of the shadow of death,[c]
   I will fear no evil,
for you are with me;
   your rod and your staff,
   they comfort me.
5 You prepare a table before me
   in the presence of my enemies;
you anoint my head with oil;
   my cup overflows.
6 Surely[d] goodness and mercy[e] shall follow me
   all the days of my life,
and I shall dwell[f] in the house of the LORD
   forever.[g]

Read Psalm 28:6–9:

[6] Blessed be the LORD!
   For he has heard the voice of my pleas for mercy.
[7] The LORD is my strength and my shield;
   in him my heart trusts, and I am helped;
my heart exults,
   and with my song I give thanks to him.
[8] The LORD is the strength of his people;[a]
   he is the saving refuge of his anointed.
[9] Oh, save your people and bless your heritage!
   Be their shepherd and carry them forever.

"I am" the resurrection.

When Jesus calls Himself the resurrection, what does that mean? What are the characteristics of the resurrection? What is required on our part to receive these characteristics in our life? Why is this so important?

Read John 11:17–27; 38–44:

I Am the Resurrection and the Life

17 Now when Jesus came, he found that Lazarus had already been in the tomb four days. 18 Bethany was near Jerusalem, about two miles[a] off, 19 and many of the Jews had come to Martha and Mary to console them concerning their brother. 20 So when Martha heard that Jesus was coming, she went and met him, but Mary remained seated in the house. 21 Martha said to Jesus, "Lord, if you had been here, my brother would not have died. 22 But even now I know that whatever you ask from God, God will give you." 23 Jesus said to her, "Your brother will rise again." 24 Martha said to him, "I know that he will rise again in the resurrection on the last day." 25 Jesus said to her, "I am the resurrection and the life.[b] Whoever believes in me, though he die, yet shall he live, 26 and everyone who lives and believes in me shall never die. Do you believe this?" 27 She said to him, "Yes, Lord; I believe that you are the Christ, the Son of God, who is coming into the world."

Jesus Raises Lazarus

38 Then Jesus, deeply moved again, came to the tomb. It was a cave, and a stone lay against it. 39 Jesus said, "Take away the stone." Martha, the sister of the dead man, said to him, "Lord, by this time there will be an odor, for he has been dead four days." 40 Jesus said to her, "Did I not tell you that if you believed you would see the glory of God?" 41 So they took away the stone. And Jesus lifted up his eyes and said, "Father, I thank you that you have heard me. 42 I knew that you always hear me, but I said this on account of the people standing around, that they may believe that you sent me." 43 When he had said these things, he cried out with a loud voice, "Lazarus, come out." 44 The man who had died came out, his hands and feet bound with linen strips, and his face wrapped with a cloth. Jesus said to them, "Unbind him, and let him go."

____

____

____

____

____

We understand the sacrifice that Christ fulfilled at the cross to give us the opportunity to have a relationship with Him. What is the significance of Him having risen? What does that mean for us? Why is this so important to our life?

Read Matthew 28:1–8:

The Resurrection

28 Now after the Sabbath, toward the dawn of the first day of the week, Mary Magdalene and the other Mary went to see the tomb. [2] And behold, there was a great earthquake, for an angel of the Lord descended from heaven and came and rolled back the stone and sat on it. [3] His appearance was like lightning, and his clothing white as snow. [4] And for fear of him the guards trembled and became like dead men. [5] But the angel said to the women, "Do not be afraid, for I know that you seek Jesus who was crucified. [6] He is not here, for he has risen, as he said. Come, see the place where he[a] lay. [7] Then go quickly and tell his disciples that he has risen from the dead, and behold, he is going before you to Galilee; there you will see him. See, I have told you." [8] So they departed quickly from the tomb with fear and great joy, and ran to tell his disciples.

____

____

____

____

____

We are raised with Christ. What does that mean? What are the four things that Christ fulfilled at His death and resurrection? How then are we to live given that these things have been fulfilled? Why is this so important for us?

Read Colossians 2:11–15:

[11] In him also you were circumcised with a circumcision made without hands, by putting off the body of the flesh, by the circumcision of Christ, [12] having been buried with him in baptism, in which you were also raised with him through faith in the powerful working of God, who raised him from the dead. [13] And you, who were dead in your trespasses and the uncircumcision of your flesh, God made alive together with him, having forgiven us all our trespasses, [14] by canceling the record of debt that stood against us with its legal demands. This he set aside, nailing it to the cross. [15] He disarmed the rulers and authorities[a] and put them to open shame, by triumphing over them in him.[b]

____

____

____

____

____

LESSON 2:
"I AM" THE RESURRECTION AND THE LIFE

How did the disciples bear witness to the resurrection? How is this different from just speaking about the truth of the resurrection? How then are we to bear witness to the resurrection? Why is this so important?

Read Acts 4:32–33:

They Had Everything in Common

32 Now the full number of those who believed were of one heart and soul, and no one said that any of the things that belonged to him was his own, but they had everything in common. 33 And with great power the apostles were giving their testimony to the resurrection of the Lord Jesus, and great grace was upon them all.

As we bear witness to the resurrection, what are the benefits to us? How are these benefits given to us? Why is this so important to how we live this life of Christ?

Read 1 Peter 1:1–12:

Greeting

1 Peter, an apostle of Jesus Christ,
To those who are elect exiles of the Dispersion in Pontus, Galatia, Cappadocia, Asia, and Bithynia, 2 according to the foreknowledge of God the Father, in the sanctification of the Spirit, for obedience to Jesus Christ and for sprinkling with his blood:

May grace and peace be multiplied to you.

Born Again to a Living Hope
3 Blessed be the God and Father of our Lord Jesus Christ! According to his great mercy, he has caused us to be born again to a living hope through the resurrection of Jesus Christ from the dead, 4 to an inheritance that is imperishable, undefiled, and unfading, kept in heaven for you, 5 who by God's power are being guarded through faith for a salvation ready to be revealed in the last time. 6 In this you rejoice, though now for a little while, if necessary, you have been grieved by various trials, 7 so that the tested genuineness of your faith—more precious than gold that perishes though it is tested by fire—may be found to result in praise and glory and honor at the revelation of Jesus Christ. 8 Though you have not seen him, you love him. Though you do not now see him, you believe in him and rejoice with joy that is inexpressible and filled with glory, 9 obtaining the outcome of your faith, the salvation of your souls. 10 Concerning this salvation, the prophets who prophesied about the grace that was to be yours searched and inquired carefully, 11 inquiring what person or time[a] the Spirit of Christ in them was indicating when he predicted the sufferings of Christ and the subsequent glories. 12 It was revealed to them that they were serving not themselves but you, in the things that have now been announced to you through those who preached the good news to you by the Holy Spirit sent from heaven, things into which angels long to look.

____

____

____

____

____

To live the life of the resurrection, it is necessary for us to walk with Him and receive all these benefits. Following the progression described here, what has Christ done to give us this opportunity, and how are we to respond to this? What is the reason we must respond this way? What are the benefits of responding this way?

Read Romans 6:1–7; 18, 22:

Dead to Sin, Alive to God
6 What shall we say then? Are we to continue in sin that grace may abound? [2] By no means! How can we who died to sin still live in it? [3] Do you not know that all of us who have been baptized into Christ Jesus were baptized into his death? [4] We were buried therefore with him by baptism into death, in order that, just as Christ was raised from the dead by the glory of the Father, we too might walk in newness of life.

[5] For if we have been united with him in a death like his, we shall certainly be united with him in a resurrection like his. [6] We know that our old self[a] was crucified with him in order that the body of sin might be brought to nothing, so that we would no longer be enslaved to sin. [7] For one who has died has been set free[b] from sin.

[18] and, having been set free from sin, have become slaves of righteousness.

[22] But now that you have been set free from sin and have become slaves of God, the fruit you get leads to sanctification and its end, eternal life.

____

____

____

____

____

As we live in the resurrection, what is God's good work in and for us? What then shall we expect our life to experience? When? Why?

> **Read Hebrews 13:20–21:**
>
> Benediction
> [20] Now may the God of peace who brought again from the dead our Lord Jesus, the great shepherd of the sheep, by the blood of the eternal covenant, [21]equip you with everything good that you may do his will, working in us[a] that which is pleasing in his sight, through Jesus Christ, to whom be glory forever and ever. Amen.

____

____

____

____

____

LESSON 3:
"I AM" THE WAY, THE TRUTH, AND THE LIFE

The Way, The Truth, and the Life:

What does it mean that Jesus is the way? In order for us to walk in His way, what must we pursue and experience? What does that mean for how we live?

> **Read John 14:6–14:**
>
> [6] Jesus said to him, "I am the way, and the truth, and the life. No one comes to the Father except through me. [7] If you had known me, you would have known my Father also.[a] From now on you do know him and have seen him."
>
> [8] Philip said to him, "Lord, show us the Father, and it is enough for us." [9] Jesus said to him, "Have I been with you so long, and you still do not know me, Philip? Whoever has seen me has seen the Father. How can you say, 'Show us the Father'? [10] Do you not believe that I am in the Father and the Father is in me? The words that I say to you I do not speak on my own authority, but the Father who dwells in me does his works. [11] Believe me that I am in the Father and the Father is in me, or else believe on account of the works themselves.
>
> [12] "Truly, truly, I say to you, whoever believes in me will also do the works that I do; and greater works than these will he do, because I am going to the Father. [13] Whatever you ask in my name, this I will do, that the Father may be glorified in the Son. [14] If you ask me[b] anything in my name, I will do it.

> **"When Jesus was asked, 'Who are you?' He said, "I am the 'I am,'" which means He is everything. He is all of God—the nature of God, the life of God, the power of God."**

LESSON 3:
"I AM" THE WAY, THE TRUTH, AND THE LIFE

If Jesus is the way, the truth, and the life, what is important then for how God guides us? What must our heart be? If we fulfill this requirement, what will the benefits be on the way? What do these mean for our everyday life? Why?

Read Psalm 25:1–15:

Teach Me Your Paths

[a] Of David.

25 To you, O LORD, I lift up my soul.
2 O my God, in you I trust;
    let me not be put to shame;
    let not my enemies exult over me.
3 Indeed, none who wait for you shall be put to shame;
    they shall be ashamed who are wantonly treacherous.
4 Make me to know your ways, O LORD;
    teach me your paths.
5 Lead me in your truth and teach me,
    for you are the God of my salvation;
    for you I wait all the day long.
6 Remember your mercy, O LORD, and your steadfast love,
    for they have been from of old.
7 Remember not the sins of my youth or my transgressions;
    according to your steadfast love remember me,
    for the sake of your goodness, O LORD!
8 Good and upright is the LORD;
    therefore he instructs sinners in the way.
9 He leads the humble in what is right,
    and teaches the humble his way.
10 All the paths of the LORD are steadfast love and faithfulness,
    for those who keep his covenant and his testimonies.
11 For your name's sake, O LORD,
    pardon my guilt, for it is great.
12 Who is the man who fears the LORD?

> Him will he instruct in the way that he should choose.
> [13] His soul shall abide in well-being,
>   and his offspring shall inherit the land.
> [14] The friendship[b] of the LORD is for those who fear him,
>   and he makes known to them his covenant.
> [15] My eyes are ever toward the LORD,
>   for he will pluck my feet out of the net.

____

____

____

____

____

If we are to walk in the way of truth, what then is our prayer? How are we to remain in this place of following? What will be the benefit to me if I remain there?

Read Psalm 43:3–4:

> [3] Send out your light and your truth;
>   let them lead me;
> let them bring me to your holy hill
>   and to your dwelling!
> [4] Then I will go to the altar of God,
>   to God my exceeding joy,
> and I will praise you with the lyre,
>   O God, my God.

____

____

____

____

LESSON 3:
"I AM" THE WAY, THE TRUTH, AND THE LIFE

Since we are in the world and will experience trouble along the way, what are we to do in this trouble? What does He then promise regarding this trouble? Why is this such an important aspect of remaining on the way?

Read Psalm 86:1–13:

Great Is Your Steadfast Love

A Prayer of David.

86 Incline your ear, O LORD, and answer me,
    for I am poor and needy.
[2] Preserve my life, for I am godly;
    save your servant, who trusts in you—you are my God.
[3] Be gracious to me, O Lord,
    for to you do I cry all the day.
[4] Gladden the soul of your servant,
    for to you, O Lord, do I lift up my soul.
[5] For you, O Lord, are good and forgiving,
    abounding in steadfast love to all who call upon you.
[6] Give ear, O LORD, to my prayer;
    listen to my plea for grace.
[7] In the day of my trouble I call upon you,
    for you answer me.
[8] There is none like you among the gods, O Lord,
    nor are there any works like yours.
[9] All the nations you have made shall come
    and worship before you, O Lord,
    and shall glorify your name.
[10] For you are great and do wondrous things;
    you alone are God.
[11] Teach me your way, O LORD,
    that I may walk in your truth;
    unite my heart to fear your name.
[12] I give thanks to you, O Lord my God, with my whole heart,

and I will glorify your name forever.
13 For great is your steadfast love toward me;
   you have delivered my soul from the depths of Sheol.

If we are walking God's way, what are all the benefits that we are assured to receive? What is our role to be able to receive these benefits? How then shall we expect life to be for us? Why?

Read Psalm 145:

Great Is the LORD

[a] A Song of Praise. Of David.
145 I will extol you, my God and King,
   and bless your name forever and ever.
2 Every day I will bless you
   and praise your name forever and ever.
3 Great is the LORD, and greatly to be praised,
   and his greatness is unsearchable.
4 One generation shall commend your works to another,
   and shall declare your mighty acts.
5 On the glorious splendor of your majesty,
   and on your wondrous works, I will meditate.
6 They shall speak of the might of your awesome deeds,
   and I will declare your greatness.
7 They shall pour forth the fame of your abundant goodness
   and shall sing aloud of your righteousness.
8 The LORD is gracious and merciful,
   slow to anger and abounding in steadfast love.

[9] The LORD is good to all,
and his mercy is over all that he has made.
[10] All your works shall give thanks to you, O LORD,
and all your saints shall bless you!
[11] They shall speak of the glory of your kingdom
and tell of your power,
[12] to make known to the children of man your[b] mighty deeds,
and the glorious splendor of your kingdom.
[13] Your kingdom is an everlasting kingdom,
and your dominion endures throughout all generations.
[The LORD is faithful in all his words
and kind in all his works.][c]
[14] The LORD upholds all who are falling
and raises up all who are bowed down.
[15] The eyes of all look to you,
and you give them their food in due season.
[16] You open your hand;
you satisfy the desire of every living thing.
[17] The LORD is righteous in all his ways
and kind in all his works.
[18] The LORD is near to all who call on him,
to all who call on him in truth.
[19] He fulfills the desire of those who fear him;
he also hears their cry and saves them.
[20] The LORD preserves all who love him,
but all the wicked he will destroy.
[21] My mouth will speak the praise of the LORD,
and let all flesh bless his holy name forever and ever.

____

____

____

____

____

The Vine:

What does "Jesus is the vine" mean? What does that provide to us? What is the relationship between the vine and the vinedresser? What does that mean for us? What is our role, and what choice do we make? What are the benefits of making this choice? Why?

Read John 15:1–8:

I Am the True Vine

15 "I am the true vine, and my Father is the vinedresser. [2] Every branch in me that does not bear fruit he takes away, and every branch that does bear fruit he prunes, that it may bear more fruit. [3] Already you are clean because of the word that I have spoken to you. [4] Abide in me, and I in you. As the branch cannot bear fruit by itself, unless it abides in the vine, neither can you, unless you abide in me. [5] I am the vine; you are the branches. Whoever abides in me and I in him, he it is that bears much fruit, for apart from me you can do nothing. [6] If anyone does not abide in me he is thrown away like a branch and withers; and the branches are gathered, thrown into the fire, and burned. [7] If you abide in me, and my words abide in you, ask whatever you wish, and it will be done for you. [8] By this my Father is glorified, that you bear much fruit and so prove to be my disciples.

As we abide in the vine, we are on God's path. We have learned that there will be trouble, loss, difficult circumstances—even those that we caused ourselves because we were not walking on His path. First, what is required for us to return to the path? Why is this so important when we are in the middle of difficulty? If we return, what does God promise? What can we then expect about the resolution to our difficulty? Why?

Read Joel 2:22–32:

22 Fear not, you beasts of the field,
   for the pastures of the wilderness are green;
the tree bears its fruit;
   the fig tree and vine give their full yield.
23 "Be glad, O children of Zion,
   and rejoice in the LORD your God,
for he has given the early rain for your vindication;
   he has poured down for you abundant rain,
   the early and the latter rain, as before.
24 "The threshing floors shall be full of grain;
   the vats shall overflow with wine and oil.
25 I will restore[a] to you the years
   that the swarming locust has eaten,
the hopper, the destroyer, and the cutter,
   my great army, which I sent among you.
26 "You shall eat in plenty and be satisfied,
   and praise the name of the LORD your God,
   who has dealt wondrously with you.
And my people shall never again be put to shame.
27 You shall know that I am in the midst of Israel,
   and that I am the LORD your God and there is none else.
And my people shall never again be put to shame.

The LORD Will Pour Out His Spirit
28 [b]"And it shall come to pass afterward,
   that I will pour out my Spirit on all flesh;
your sons and your daughters shall prophesy,
   your old men shall dream dreams,

and your young men shall see visions.
²⁹ Even on the male and female servants
in those days I will pour out my Spirit.

³⁰ "And I will show wonders in the heavens and on the earth, blood and fire and columns of smoke. ³¹ The sun shall be turned to darkness, and the moon to blood, before the great and awesome day of the LORD comes. ³² And it shall come to pass that everyone who calls on the name of the LORD shall be saved. For in Mount Zion and in Jerusalem there shall be those who escape, as the Lord has said, and among the survivors shall be those whom the LORD calls.

As in Joel, God promises to restore to us what is lost. What are the four things He promises, and what do they mean in our practical lives? What then are our three responsibilities to receive these promises? What do each look like in our practical lives? If we fulfill this and receive these promises, what will we experience as part of God's bigger story? Why is this so important?

Read Zechariah 8:11–23:

¹¹ But now I will not deal with the remnant of this people as in the former days, declares the LORD of hosts. ¹² For there shall be a sowing of peace. The vine shall give its fruit, and the ground shall give its produce, and the heavens shall give their dew. And I will cause the remnant of this people to possess all these things. ¹³ And as you have been a byword of cursing among the nations, O house of Judah and house of Israel, so will I save you, and you shall be a blessing. Fear not, but let your hands be strong."

¹⁴ For thus says the LORD of hosts: "As I purposed to bring disaster to you when your fathers provoked me to wrath, and I did not relent, says the LORD of hosts, ¹⁵ so again have I purposed in these days to bring good to Jerusalem and to the house of Judah; fear not. ¹⁶ These are the things that you shall do: Speak the truth to one another; render in your gates judgments that are true and make for peace; ¹⁷ do not devise evil in your hearts against one another, and love no false oath, for all these things I hate, declares the LORD."

¹⁸ And the word of the LORD of hosts came to me, saying, ¹⁹ "Thus says the LORD of hosts: The fast of the fourth month and the fast of the fifth and the fast of the seventh and the fast of the tenth shall be to the house of Judah seasons of joy and gladness and cheerful feasts. Therefore love truth and peace.

²⁰ "Thus says the LORD of hosts: Peoples shall yet come, even the inhabitants of many cities. ²¹ The inhabitants of one city shall go to another, saying, 'Let us go at once to entreat the favor of the LORD and to seek the LORD of hosts; I myself am going.' ²² Many peoples and strong nations shall come to seek the LORD of hosts in Jerusalem and to entreat the favor of the LORD. ²³ Thus says the LORD of hosts: In those days ten men from the nations of every tongue shall take hold of the robe of a Jew, saying, 'Let us go with you, for we have heard that God is with you.'"